W9-BAI-399

SPORTS GREAT MARIO LEMIEUX

—Sports Great Books—

Sports Great Jim Abbott
(ISBN 0-89490-395-0)

Sports Great Troy Aikman
(ISBN 0-89490-593-7)

Sports Great Charles Barkley
(ISBN 0-89490-386-1)

Sports Great Larry Bird
(ISBN 0-89490-368-3)

Sports Great Barry Bonds
(ISBN 0-89490-595-3)

Sports Great Bobby Bonilla
(ISBN 0-89490-417-5)

Sports Great Will Clark
(ISBN 0-89490-390-X)

Sports Great Roger Clemens
(ISBN 0-89490-284-9)

Sports Great John Elway
(ISBN 0-89490-282-2)

Sports Great Patrick Ewing
(ISBN 0-89490-369-1)

Sports Great Steffi Graf
(ISBN 0-89490-597-X)

Sports Great Orel Hershiser
(ISBN 0-89490-389-6)

Sports Great Bo Jackson
(ISBN 0-89490-281-4)

**Sports Great Magic Johnson
(Revised and Expanded)**
(ISBN 0-89490-348-9)

Sports Great Michael Jordan
(ISBN 0-89490-370-5)

Sports Great Mario Lemieux
(ISBN 0-89490-596-1)

Sports Great Karl Malone
(ISBN 0-89490-599-6)

Sports Great Kevin Mitchell
(ISBN 0-89490-388-8)

Sports Great Joe Montana
(ISBN 0-89490-371-3)

Sports Great Hakeem Olajuwon
(ISBN 0-89490-372-1)

Sports Great Shaquille O'Neal
(ISBN 0-89490-594-5)

Sports Great Kirby Puckett
(ISBN 0-89490-392-6)

Sports Great Jerry Rice
(ISBN 0-89490-419-1)

Sports Great Cal Ripken, Jr.
(ISBN 0-89490-387-X)

Sports Great David Robinson
(ISBN 0-89490-373-X)

Sports Great Nolan Ryan
(ISBN 0-89490-394-2)

Sports Great Barry Sanders
(ISBN 0-89490-418-3)

Sports Great John Stockton
(ISBN 0-89490-598-8)

Sports Great Darryl Strawberry
(ISBN 0-89490-291-1)

Sports Great Isiah Thomas
(ISBN 0-89490-374-8)

Sports Great Herschel Walker
(ISBN 0-89490-207-5)

SPORTS GREAT MARIO LEMIEUX

Ron Knapp

—Sports Great Books—

ENSLOW PUBLISHERS, INC.

44 Fadem Road	P.O. Box 38
Box 699	Aldershot
Springfield, N.J. 07081	Hants GU12 6BP
U.S.A.	U.K.

Copyright © 1995 by Ron Knapp

All rights reserved.

No part of this book may be reproduced by any means
without the written permission of the publisher.

Library of Congress Cataloging-in-Publication Data
Knapp, Ron.
    Sports great Mario Lemieux / Ron Knapp.
      p. cm. — (Sports great books)
    Includes index.
    ISBN 0-89490-596-1
    1. Lemieux, Mario, 1965- —Juvenile literature. 2. Hockey
players—Canada—Biography—Juvenile literature. 3. Pittsburgh Penguins (Hockey
team)—Juvenile literature. [1. Lemieux, Mario, 1965- . 2. Hockey players.] I. Title. II. Series.
GV848.5.L46K63 1995
796.962'092—dc20
[B]

                                      94-21990
                                          CIP
                                          AC

Printed in the United States of America

10 9 8 7 6 5 4 3 2 1

Illustration Credits: Hockey Hall of Fame and Museum, pp. 15, 20, 25, 42;
Mitchell Layton Photography, pp. 8, 10, 12, 28, 30, 32, 36, 38, 46, 48, 50, 52, 55,
56, 58.

Cover Photo: Mitchell Layton Photography.

15.95

Contents

Chapter 1 . . . . *7*

Chapter 2 . . . . *13*

Chapter 3 . . . . *19*

Chapter 4 . . . . *27*

Chapter 5 . . . . *35*

Chapter 6 . . . . *45*

Chapter 7 . . . . *53*

Career Statistics *61*

Where to Write *61*

Index *63*

Chapter 1

Mario Lemieux was back!

His injured back had finally healed and he was once again on the ice for the Pittsburgh Penguins. On January 26, 1991, after missing the first fifty games of the season, he was ready to play. That night he got three assists against the Nordiques in Quebec, and the Penguins won, 6–5.

Three nights later, in Pittsburgh, the Washington Capitals took an early 2–0 lead. But then Lemieux stole the puck, tapping it to Mark Recchi. Along with Bob Errey, Mario and Recchi charged toward the Washington net. Recchi passed back to Lemieux, who knocked the puck in front of Errey, setting up an easy goal.

Still in the first period, Mario blocked a Capital shot with his leg, giving it to teammate Jaromir Jagr. Seconds later, Jagr gave the puck back to Lemieux, who tied the game 2–2 with his first goal of the year.

Penguin Phil Bourque was amazed. "I can't believe that a guy could be off that long and play like that," he said. "It must

7

After months of recovery, Mario Lemieux returned to the ice with a fury.

be a great feeling to know you can take total control of a game."

John Cullen, a former teammate, was impressed with Mario's courage and determination. "Just to see him out there in his equipment, moving around, gives you chills," he said. With their superstar back, Cullen knew that the Penguins were going to be tough. "Imagine missing the best player in the world. And now he's skating."

The Penguins finally finished off the Capitals that night in Pittsburgh when Paul Stanton's overtime goal clinched a 3–2 victory. They continued rolling through the closing weeks of the regular season, finishing first with a 41-33-6 record. Mario had 19 goals in 26 games.

In the playoffs, Pittsburgh beat the New Jersey Devils, the Washington Capitals, and the Boston Bruins, setting up a finals confrontation with the Minnesota North Stars. The Penguins lost the opener, 5–4, before taking a 2–1 lead in the next game. That's when Lemieux headed for the net with the puck. Shawn Chambers tried to block his way, but Mario slipped the puck between the defenseman's skates, skidded past him, took control of the puck again, and started picking up speed. He faked a shot to bring goalie Jon Casey out of the net. Then with Casey out of position, Lemieux popped in the goal. Pittsburgh finally won 4–1, evening the series at one game apiece.

After the game, teammate Kevin Stevens reminded reporters of Lemieux's courage. "People don't know how bad his injury was," he said. "He had to lie in bed for seven or eight weeks and now he's come back like this. He's got guys on him all night and he's getting hit all the time."

All that punishment on the ice seemed to be taking its toll on Lemieux. Before the third game, the pain in his back had returned. The doctors said that he now had back spasms. The

9

The pain from the return of his back spasms showed on Mario Lemieux's face.

muscles kept tightening and loosening, making it impossible for him to play. Without him, Pittsburgh lost, 3–1.

But Lemieux returned to action for Game Four. He picked up a goal and an assist as the Penguins won, 5–3. Then, in Game Five, Recchi got two goals to give them a 6–4 victory. One more win and Pittsburgh would have its first Stanley Cup.

In that game, Lemieux took a pass off the wall and shot it in to give the Penguins a 2–0 lead. After that, the game was theirs. Mario's teammates kept pouring in goals, and Pittsburgh won, 8–0. Lemieux and his team had won their first Stanley Cup! He had earned the Conn Smythe Trophy as the most valuable player of the playoffs, with 16 goals and 28 assists in 23 games.

It had been an incredible season, beginning with Mario in a hospital bed and ending with him skating around the rink in triumph, holding the Stanley Cup over his head.

The Penguins and their fans were delighted, of course, that Lemieux was back in uniform. And just the sight of him on the ice gave chills to the goalies of the National Hockey League. With his skates and equipment, Mario stood 6 feet 7 inches and weighed well over 200 pounds. His long, powerful arms had been compared to the wings of the pterodactyl, the flying dinosaur. He used them to steal the puck and thread his way through defensemen. Dave Gagner of the Minnesota North Stars said, "When somebody that big and that good wants to win that badly, there isn't much you can do."

In French, Mario's native language, "le mieux" means "the best." The Pittsburgh fans figured that that was exactly what he was.

11

Mario Lemieux helped bring the Pittsburgh Penguins their first ever Stanley Cup.

Chapter 2

Mario Lemieux was born in Montreal, Quebec (Kwi-BEK), on October 5, 1965. His parents were Jean-Guy, a construction worker, and Pierrette, a housewife. Mario had two older brothers, Alain and Richard.

Montreal is the biggest city in Quebec, one of Canada's ten provinces. Quebec is at the northeastern corner of the North American continent, north of the states of New York, Vermont, New Hampshire, and Maine.

Quebec's first European settlers were French fur traders who came to the region more than 300 years ago. The area was known as New France until English troops won the Battle of Quebec in 1759. After that, all of Canada became part of the British Empire. It wasn't until 1867 that the Dominion of Canada became a separate country.

Even today, more than 200 years after the Battle of Quebec, the people of the province are very proud of their heritage. They don't want to lose their French cultural identity. Some would like Quebec to be separate from Canada and become a country of its own. Almost all Quebec's inhabitants, including the Lemieux family, speak French. Almost everybody else in all of the other nine provinces speaks English. Since Canada is a bilingual country, all of its notices, road signs, and money are printed in both languages. Mario himself did not learn to speak English well until he was already a star in Pittsburgh.

But no matter what language they speak, almost all Canadians seem to love ice hockey. The Lemieux home on Rue Jorgue in the Ville Emard neighborhood of Montreal is within walking distance of the Forum, home of the Montreal Canadiens, one of the best teams in the National Hockey League. Mario's father, Jean-Guy, usually had a season ticket every year.

Like many other Canadian boys, Mario and his brothers learned to skate almost as soon as they could walk. There was a rink across the street behind St. Jean de Matha Church, but when they were little Mrs. Lemieux didn't want the boys crossing the street by themselves, so she decided that they needed a rink of their own. During the cold Quebec winters, she had always washed the carpets in her home with fresh snow and that gave her an idea. She and her husband carried snow into a hallway of the house, packed it down, and turned the hall into an indoor rink. "The boys were so young that they were skating more on the boots than on the blades, but it was fun," Mrs. Lemieux said. "I would have played too if I could have." Sometimes the boys let her play goalie.

After a few years of indoor hockey, the Lemieux brothers were old enough to cross the street by themselves. They began spending almost all their time on the rink behind the church. They usually didn't stop playing hockey until 9 or 10 o'clock at night.

Mario joined his first team when he was only six. On his jersey he wore number 27, the same as his big brother Alain.

Hockey is the most popular professional sport in Canada. Most of the greatest National Hockey League stars, including Mario, have been Canadians.

Right away, he was hard to miss. He was big for his age, and already he knew how to move the puck around the ice. Even as a child he played hard. When he didn't win, he got mad. "If Mario lost," Mr. Lemieux said, "it would be as if a hurricane went through the basement."

One of the most popular television programs in Canada is "Hockey Night in Canada," a weekly game featuring NHL teams on Saturday nights. The Lemieux brothers always made sure to quit practice early so they could watch. When Mario was eight, his parents left Alain, Richard, and Mario with a baby-sitter. There was no trouble until she switched the channel from "Hockey Night in Canada" to a movie she wanted to watch. The boys couldn't believe it. How could anybody turn off a hockey game? They solved the problem by locking the baby-sitter inside the bathroom. When she yelled at them, they just turned up the volume on the television set.

Ron Stevenson was Mario's coach from the time he was ten until he was fourteen, and still remembers Mario's first game. The Ville Emard Hurricanes were going against the Notre Dame de Grace Maroons, the roughest team in the league. "The NDG Maroons were rough and hit hard," said Stevenson, "but they couldn't even touch him. He got eight goals."

Even though he was still quite young, Mario was a very dedicated player. He put in a lot of extra practice time. Over and over he went through the same drills with his teammates. Once his mother called Stevenson to tell him that Mario wouldn't be coming to practice because he was sick. But a few hours later he was out on the ice, skating with the rest of the team. "I had to bring him," Mrs. Lemieux said. "He was breaking up the house."

Mario hated to make mistakes on the rink. Stevenson had his players write sentences like "I must not take bad penalties" one hundred times. Mario assigned himself punishment sentences like "I must work harder on back-checking." Stevenson says that he never had any trouble with his star player. Mario enjoyed his four years with the coach. Besides hockey skills, the most important thing he learned from Stevenson was to be polite. Like some other teenagers, Mario would sometimes be rude to adults. That kind of behavior wasn't tolerated by his coach.

But Mario's polite attitude isn't what made him well known throughout Quebec. The Hurricanes played more than 75 games a year. Thousands of hockey fans were watching and reading about the hotshot young player from Ville Emard. Three times he led his team to the Quebec provincial championship. Usually he was the league scoring champ, too.

Even as a youngster, Mario was discovering that hockey was a rugged sport. He had to be willing to take more than a few bumps and bruises. When he was twelve he scored 12 points in a game at a tournament in Ottawa, Ontario. After the game, Stevenson found him relaxing in the shower. "With just a towel around him, he looked like a beaten child," Stevenson said. "He had two black eyes . . . slashes and marks all over his body. It was brutal."

Already Mario was thinking about a career in the NHL. Of course, playing professional hockey is the dream of most young players, but Mario knew he was good enough to have a shot at making his dream come true. He could hardly wait until he was old enough.

Mario Lemieux was born in Montreal, Quebec. Montreal is the largest city in the province, but Quebec is the capital. French is the official language of the Canadian province of Quebec.

Chapter 3

When Mario Lemieux finished playing on Ron Stevenson's team, he was known throughout Quebec as a great hockey player, but he wasn't ready yet for the National Hockey League. After all, he was still only fourteen years old.

The next season (1980–81) he played for the Montreal team in the Midget Triple A League. Once again wearing number 27, he was one of the best players. He could move quickly and gracefully all over the ice, and he always seemed to know exactly where the puck was going to be. He was also still growing. That year he scored 62 goals, a league record.

Mario was already being compared to hockey greats like Guy Lafleur, Montreal's veteran scoring champ, and Wayne Gretzky, Edmonton's young superstar. Lemieux and Gretzky met for the first time in Toronto. By then Gretzky was already winning scoring titles in the NHL. He told Mario to continue working hard and not to get upset about all the attention he was getting in the newspapers.

Then he was offered a contract by the Laval Voisins in the Quebec Major Junior Hockey League (QMJHL). He would be

Lemieux in his Laval Voisins uniform.

paid about thirty-five dollars a week. It wasn't much, but the contract meant that he was a step closer to the NHL. When Mario signed with Laval, he promised that he would lead the team to a championship.

Players in the QMJHL hope to play well enough to be noticed by major league teams. Their goal is always to make it to the majors. Each summer the NHL conducts a draft in which the teams take turns picking new players. Athletes good enough to be chosen are offered pro contracts worth thousands and even millions of dollars.

Signing with the Voisins meant two changes for Lemieux. First, for at least part of the season he would be away from his family, living in a boardinghouse in Laval. The Lemieux family was a close one, and Mario didn't enjoy being away from his parents and brothers. Since he was usually shy and quiet, it was not easy for him to make friends.

When he joined Laval, Mario decided to change his number. Ever since he had begun playing, he had worn number 27 in honor of his brother Alain. For a while he considered copying Gretzky and wearing 99, but then he decided that he wanted a number of his own. Finally Mario settled on 66. Turn it over and it's easy to figure out who his hero was. Already Lemieux was hoping that his 66 would one day be as famous as Gretzky's 99.

During his first season (1981–82) in the QMJHL, Mario scored only 30 goals. With his 66 assists, that gave him 96 points. He didn't come close to winning the league scoring title, and Laval didn't take the championship. Some of the fans were disappointed. They wondered if Lemieux might be just another player.

He was only sixteen, but already under a great deal of pressure. He was a professional player and all his games were thoroughly covered by newspapers, radio, and television. People forgot that he was still just a kid.

Mario responded to the pressure by deciding to devote all his attention and energy to hockey. He told his parents that he was going to quit school. "I wanted to be able to skate in the morning and play hockey at night without being tired for the game, and I figured I could do my learning through living and traveling," he said. For a while Mr. Lemieux tried to convince his son to remain in school. "Finally he agreed with me that I should concentrate on hockey because I was only two years away from the draft."

Whether it was the result of quitting school or simply getting used to the pressure, Mario did much better in 1982–83. He had 84 goals and 100 assists for 184 points. He probably would have won the league scoring title if he hadn't missed several games in the middle of the season in order to compete on Canada's team in the World Junior Championships in Moscow. During the tournament, however, Mario watched most of the action from the bench. The coach said he wasn't good enough to earn a spot on the ice. Mario was angry. Why had he wasted his time going to Moscow? If he wasn't good enough to play, why hadn't the coach just let him stay behind in Laval?

While he was in Moscow, Mario was passed in the scoring statistics by Verdun's Pat LaFontaine, the same player who would battle him for the NHL title ten years later.

By the time Lemieux started his final year with Laval in 1983, he was easily the best player in the QMJHL. He was big and strong and fast and tricky. It was very hard for the defenders to keep up with him. He used his long arms and legs to slip around them or he used his strength to blast right through them. His opponents decided that the only way to stop him was to play dirty. They followed him up and down the ice, bumping him with their elbows and slashing and hooking him with their sticks. That made Mario angry. He always figured he had the skills and the determination to win by playing fairly. He expected the men who guarded him to do the same. During one game he finally got tired of the bumps, hooks, and slashes. He threw off his gloves and punched the player who had been after him. Of course, he was sent to the penalty box for fighting, but after that the other players gave him a little more room.

There was no doubt about Lemieux's talent after the 1983–84 season. Fans from all over Canada came to watch him play. All the tickets to every game were sold out. Even NHL players Guy Lafleur and Wayne Gretzky showed up. With only one game left, Mario had 127 goals, just two short of Lafleur's record set in 1970–71 when he was a junior player. Could Lemieux break the record? No problem. He scored six goals and five assists that night. After the game he was doing a victory dance under the stands when Gretzky congratulated him.

Lemieux finished the season with 133 goals, 149 assists, and 282 points, all league records. That gave him a three-year career total of 247 goals, 315 assists, and 562 points, more league records.

But not everything went perfectly for Mario in his final season in junior hockey. He caused a controversy by turning down a chance to play for Canada in the World Junior Hockey Championships in Sweden. He still remembered sitting on the bench in Moscow. He didn't want to miss part of the season with Laval again. Besides, the tournament started on Christmas Day, when he wanted to be home with his parents and brothers.

Because he wouldn't play for his country's team, many Canadians thought he was unpatriotic. They felt that it was his duty to go to Sweden. Mario disagreed. When the league suspended him for skipping the tournament, he went to court. The judge agreed that he had the right to refuse to go to Sweden, and he ordered the QMJHL to lift the suspension.

Back on the ice, Lemieux failed in his promise to bring a championship to Laval. In the Memorial Cup playoffs, he played poorly and the Voisins were eliminated. Once again his detractors complained. He didn't like to play hard, they said, and he couldn't win the big games. Many of them wondered if he was tough enough to make it in the NHL.

Eddie Johnston wasn't worried. He was the general manager of the Pittsburgh Penguins, the worst team in the NHL. They had won only 16 out of 80 games during the 1983–84 season. Because the Penguins had the worst record in the league, they would get the first pick in the 1984 summer draft. Johnston had no doubt who he would choose. He wanted Lemieux.

Well before the draft the Penguin general manager had begun negotiating a contract with Mario's agents, Gus Badali and Bob Perno, but they weren't making much progress because Pittsburgh wasn't willing to pay Lemieux what he felt he was worth. When the draft was held in Montreal they still hadn't reached an agreement. Mario and his family were sitting in the stands when the Penguins announced that he was their choice. He stood up and waved. A Penguin representative told him to come down so that he could put on one of their jerseys. Mario thought the man was being rude. He sat down and told him, "Don't tell me what to do when you don't want to pay me what I'm worth."

The Pittsburgh fans were outraged. They figured he ought to be happy that he was drafted first. He should have been proud to put on the Penguin jersey. But Mario was stubborn,

24

After tough contract negotiations, Mario agreed to wear the uniform of the Pittsburgh Penguins. As part of the settlement, the Penguins agreed to install a satellite dish on Mario's parents' house.

and he thought he was right. "I'm not afraid to stand up to them," he said.

Five days later, Lemieux and his agents finally agreed to sign with the Penguins. He would be paid $700,000 for two years, an incredible amount of money for an 18-year-old who had been making thirty-five dollars a week playing junior hockey. The contract was a complicated document. Mario would get a $150,000 bonus as soon as he signed. If the Penguins averaged 10,000 fans a game, he would get extra money. The team also promised to put a satellite dish on the Lemieux home in Ville Emard so that his family could watch all his games.

Mario used one of his first paychecks to buy his father a new Pontiac automobile. Then he prepared to move to a new career in a new country—the United States—and a new city—Pittsburgh, Pennsylvania.

Chapter 4

When Mario Lemieux came to Pittsburgh in 1984, he was still only nineteen. He was hundreds of miles away from his family and his girlfriend, Nathalie Asselin, whom he'd met during his last year with Laval. His English was still poor, and hardly anybody in Pittsburgh spoke French. It could have been a miserable, lonely year.

Luckily for Lemieux, the Penguins had arranged for him to stay with a local family, Tom and Nancy Matthews and their three teenaged sons. Mario and the Matthews family got along very well. They helped him settle into his new country. Soon neighbors weren't surprised to see him on the street with the Matthews boys, knocking a ball around with a hockey stick.

During his first months in Pittsburgh, reporters had a rough time interviewing him. Many times he didn't understand their English questions, so he just said "yes" or "no." To make it easier to communicate, he began carrying an English-French dictionary. He spent a lot of time looking up the words he wanted to say. But he later said that what

Pittsburgh was a strange new city for the young Mario Lemieux. While it was hard to adjust, the Penguins helped make it easier.

improved his English the most wasn't living with the Matthews family or studying his dictionary. He learned to speak English well by watching American soap operas on television.

Lemieux was once again under a lot of pressure. He had just signed the richest rookie contract in the history of the league, and the Penguin fans expected him to earn all that money by bringing a Stanley Cup championship to Pittsburgh. If he didn't bring in thousands of new fans, the Penguins might be finished. The team might go bankrupt or have to move to another city. Mario knew that the team and city were counting on him.

He scored a goal the first time he was on the ice, then added 42 more before the season was over. He also got 57 assists. To determine scoring statistics, goals and assists are combined as points. With 43 goals and 57 assists, Mario had 100 points. That was 108 behind Wayne Gretzky's league-leading total, but it wasn't bad for a rookie. In fact, only two rookies, Peter Stastny and Dale Hawerchuk, had ever done better. That year Lemieux received the Calder Memorial Trophy as rookie of the year.

In 1985, Gretzky's great year had led the Edmonton Oilers to their second straight Stanley Cup title. Meanwhile, Mario's Penguins were still in last place of the Patrick Division of the Prince of Wales Conference. Their record was 24-51-5. That was only eight more victories than the previous year—without Lemieux. But the Pittsburgh fans were patient. They could see that the team was improving. They were confident that in a few years Mario's team would be battling Gretzky's for the Stanley Cup. Average attendance at games that season jumped more than 4,000 to 10,018.

After the season, Lemieux admitted, "It was tough. There was a lot of pressure, playing against older guys with a lot

29

Wayne Gretzky, now a star with the Los Angeles Kings, was the star of the Edmonton Oilers when Lemieux began his rookie year in 1984. That season Gretzky would lead the Oilers to their second straight Stanley Cup.

more experience. But it went pretty well and I thought I had some pretty good games."

Mario's best performance probably came in that year's All-Star Game in Calgary, Alberta. Playing against the NHL's greatest stars, he broke open a tight game with a third-period goal. His team, the Wales Conference, won 6–4, and he was named the game's Most Valuable Player. His prize was a Chevy Blazer, which he gave to his brother Richard, who was by then a grocer back in Montreal.

By 1985 his opponents were glad to realize that Lemieux had finally stopped growing. He was 6 feet 4 inches and 212 pounds. That made him one of the biggest players in the league.

When the season ended, he reluctantly agreed to compete with Team Canada in an international tournament in Prague, Czechoslovakia. He would rather have relaxed by playing golf and watching television, but he didn't want to hear any more complaints about his patriotism.

Almost as soon as he got to Prague, Mario pulled a groin muscle, so for a few games he was unable to play. Once he *could* play, he led Canada to an upset victory over the Union of Soviet Socialist Republics (USSR). Team Canada surprised almost everybody by taking second place in the tournament. In turn, Lemieux was surprised by how much he had enjoyed himself. He said he would be glad to participate in other international competitions.

Back with the Penguins for the 1985–86 season, Mario raised his goal total to 48. His 93 assists gave him 141 points, second only to Gretzky's record-breaking 215. It was the fifth consecutive season that "The Great One" had taken the scoring title. He also won his sixth straight Hart Memorial Trophy as Most Valuable Player. But the players surprised almost everybody by picking Lemieux as the league's

At 6 feet 4 inches and 212 pounds, Lemieux had grown by 1985 into one of the biggest players in the National Hockey League.

outstanding player. For that, he received the Lester B. Pearson Award.

Gretzky's Oilers were knocked out of the playoffs early, and the Stanley Cup was eventually won by the Montreal Canadiens. Pittsburgh had its best record since 1978–79, winning 34 games. But the Penguins' fifth-place finish wasn't good enough to earn them a spot in the playoffs.

The Penguin fans were still patient and confident. Average attendance increased to 12,576. There was no doubt who they were paying to see. Lemieux was making hockey popular once more in Pittsburgh. Just having him around was making his teammates play better. Terry Ruskowski got 26 goals, his best ever. He gave the credit to his superstar teammate. "You have to be ready for a pass when Mario has the puck because he has such a great touch," he said. When the defenders closed in on Lemieux, he would often send a beautiful pass Ruskowski's way. Eddie Johnston, the team's general manager, said, "He means at least a point and a half or two points a game for us. When he's out there, he upgrades the skills of everybody else."

Each year a Pittsburgh newspaper awards the "Dapper Dan Award" to the athlete voted by fans as the most popular in the city. In 1986, Mario was the first hockey player to win.

An article in *Sports Illustrated* summed up Mario's first two years in Pittsburgh: "No player—not Wayne Gretzky, not Bobby Orr—has ever been asked to do so much both on the ice and off. No player has ever responded more brilliantly and gracefully."

Lemieux's initial contract with the Penguins covered only his first two seasons. After another long series of negotiations, his agents and the team management agreed on a new one. He would be paid $2.75 million over the next five seasons. It was

33

the second richest contract in hockey. Only Gretzky would be making more money.

As he sat with his father and Bob Perno, his agent, in the Penguins' office waiting to sign the contract and become one of the richest twenty-year-olds in the world, Mario had other things on his mind. He challenged Perno to a football match on a video-game hookup. He seemed to be more interested in the video game than in signing the big contract.

Chapter 5

Mario Lemieux missed seventeen games during the 1986–87 season, most of them because of a sprained knee. But late in the season, as Pittsburgh battled for a spot in the playoffs, he came down with bronchitis, a lung disease. Instead of being on the ice, he was in the hospital. Mario soon recovered, but by then it was too late. The Penguins had finished in fifth place and missed the playoffs once again.

Despite his health problems, Mario had made 54 goals, his best total so far, but he only got 53 assists for 107 points. That put him in third place behind Wayne Gretzky's 183 and Jari Kurri's 108. Once again Gretzky won the Hart Memorial Trophy and Lester B. Pearson Award as the league's most valuable player. But when the fans got to choose an all-star team to face the Union of Soviet Socialist Republics in February 1987, Lemieux and not Gretzky was the starting center. That was a sign of the growing respect Mario was earning across the league.

In September 1987, Mario and the rest of the NHL's best players again faced the Soviets in the finals of the Canada Cup

35

When NHL fans elected Lemieux to Team Canada, it was a sign of the growing respect he was earning for his play.

tournament. This time Gretzky was the starting center and Lemieux was moved to right wing. They were on the same line, which meant they were on the ice together. It was easy for Mario to see why many people considered Gretzky the greatest player in the history of the game. "Every shift, every time we were on the ice, Wayne tried to do the impossible," he said.

The Great One was also impressed. "Mario picked everybody up, including me," he said. "Mario and I were playing out of instinct. We think the same things, go to the same holes, see everything the same way." Lemieux and Gretzky couldn't be stopped. Mario had 11 goals, nine of them off assists by Gretzky. Team Canada won the tournament.

Playing for the 1987 Canada Cup was one of the best things that ever happened to Lemieux. He scored more goals than anybody, but more important than that, he had a chance to work closely with Gretzky and other stars, and to see that he could hold his own against the best hockey players in the world. "Playing alongside Wayne gave me a lot of confidence in myself," he said. "And I brought it back to Pittsburgh."

Lemieux led the Penguins to their first winning season in nine years. His most impressive performance probably came in the All-Star Game in St. Louis. After picking up two goals and three assists, his team, the Wales Conference, was tied with the Campbell Conference 5–5 when regulation time ran out. In overtime, he closed in on the goalie by faking his way past a defenseman, then ended the game with a flick shot into the net.

Despite a winning record (36-35-9), the Penguins again failed to qualify for the playoffs. But Mario's 70 goals, 98 assists, and 168 points were good enough to beat Gretzky and everybody else for the scoring title. It was the first time since

37

Lemieux sneaks behind the goal, and moves the puck past a defenseman during the All-Star Game. Mario's overtime goal won the 1987 All-Star Game.

1981 (when Mario was fourteen years old) that anybody but the Great One had taken the Art Ross Trophy. Lemieux also won the Hart Memorial Trophy as MVP, the first time Gretzky hadn't won it since 1979–80.

As Mario watched Gretzky's Oilers win another Stanley Cup, he couldn't wait for the 1988–89 season to begin. Sure, he enjoyed the trophies and the individual honors, but he wanted to play on a championship team, too. "I'd give up all the personal achievements to be in the playoffs," he said.

So that he would be in top condition he gave up smoking. He had only smoked a few cigarettes a day, but he knew that that was enough to cut down his endurance in the long, tough games. It was also a poor example for all his young fans. For years, he had been telling them to stay away from habits that would hurt their health. "We couldn't play hockey if we took drugs," he said. "The game's too fast. We couldn't survive."

By now Mario was probably the most popular man in Pittsburgh. A Montreal paper said he was *"Le roi de Pittsburgh"*—"the king of Pittsburgh." He was living in an apartment of his own now, a few miles from the Civic Arena where the Penguins played. Of course, he made many trips back to Ville Emard, and he still spent a lot of time with his family and his girlfriend, Nathalie Asselin.

The Penguins had realized that they couldn't be a one-man team. To make it to the playoffs they needed good players to support Lemieux. So they began picking up people like defenseman Paul Coffey, goalie Tom Barrasso, and backup center Rob Brown. The Penguin fans thought they could see a Stanley Cup in their team's future. It was getting harder and harder to find an empty place in the 16,000-seat Civic Center.

At the beginning of the 1988–89 season, Pittsburgh was the hottest team in the NHL. Lemieux collected 40 points in the first 12 games. His fans began dreaming of a 300-point season as well as a Stanley Cup. Halfway through the season, Mario had 100 points and the Penguins were leading the Patrick Division.

The team cooled off a bit after that, but Lemieux still won the scoring title with 85 goals, 114 assists, and 199 points. The Penguins dropped to second place, but that was still good enough to qualify for the playoffs.

In the first round, Pittsburgh dusted off the New York Rangers in four straight games. Then they split the first four games of the division finals against the Philadelphia Flyers. In the fourth game, however, Mario had to leave the ice with a sprained neck after bumping heads with teammate Randy Cunneyworth. Nobody was sure how soon he could play again.

But after two days of rest he was able to skate out onto the rink for the fifth game on April 25, 1989. His teammates feared the injury might keep him from playing at his best. They needn't have worried. Barely two minutes into the game, Lemieux broke away from the defenders and backhanded the puck into the net. "Once I got the first goal," he said later, "I thought we could have a big night." He was right.

Less than two minutes later he slapped in a long shot. Then less than three minutes after that, he scored again, this time on a quick wrist shot. Just seven minutes into the game, he had a hat trick and the Penguins led 3–0.

Lemieux got his fourth goal in the second period when he stole the puck from goalie Ron Hextall and poked it back into the net. Late in the game he finished the scoring by knocking in his fifth goal. Pittsburgh won, 10–3, and led the series, 3–2. Mario's 5 goals tied a playoff record. His 3 assists gave him 8 points, to tie another record.

Unfortunately for the Penguins, that was the last game they would win. Philadelphia took the next two games, 6–2 and 4–1, and Pittsburgh was eliminated. Even though he had won the scoring title and would soon be named Player of the Year by *The Sporting News*, Mario was disappointed that once again there would be no Stanley Cup for the Penguins.

Early in the season, on November 30, 1988, he had signed a one-year contract with Pittsburgh for $1.9 million. Then, after the season was over, he settled on a five-year contract good for $10 million.

By now, fans were calling Mario "Le Magnifique," The Magnificent. After a relatively slow start in 1989–90, he again took over the scoring lead from Gretzky. After 56 games, he had 43 goals, 77 assists, and 120 points. The Great One had 29, 78, and 107. The Penguins were in second place, and it looked as if they'd be able to make another run at the Stanley Cup.

But there was something seriously wrong with Mario. He went to the doctors complaining about a backache that wouldn't go away, and they said he had herniated disks. The backbone is made up of a series of twenty-six small bones, called vertebrae, which are separated and cushioned by spongy tissues called disks. One of his disks had been squashed between a pair of vertebrae. No wonder his back hurt so badly. It was hard to believe that he had just had a 46-game scoring streak. How many points could he have gotten if he had been healthy?

For a while Mario tried to play with a back brace. The trainer adjusted it almost every time he came off the ice, but it was no use. He was in so much pain that he couldn't play any more. He couldn't even bend over to lace up his skates. He missed 21 of the last 22 games, and Pittsburgh fell to fifth place, out of contention for the playoffs. Lemieux lost the scoring race to Gretzky, now playing for the Los Angeles Kings.

41

Lemieux was leading the league in scoring when he again began having back problems. Going into the 1990–91 season, his doctors were unsure he would ever play again.

Rest wasn't healing Mario's back. Doctors decided that the only way to fix the problem was to operate. In July, he had the operation and the damaged portion of the disk was removed. By October, he was able to skate again, and there was hope that he would be able to play in a few weeks.

But the pain came back, worse than ever. Mario had to quit skating. His back hurt so badly that it was hard for him even to walk. Then the doctors discovered a new problem. Lemieux was suffering from a severe infection in his lower back. The only way to cure it was for him to rest and take antibiotics.

As the Penguins began the 1990–91 season without him, Mario spent most of his time in bed. Nobody knew when—or if—he would ever be able to play hockey again.

Chapter 6

Even without Mario Lemieux, the Pittsburgh Penguins had become a strong team in 1990. They were scoring more goals than any other team in the National Hockey League. More importantly, they were near the top of the standings in the Patrick Division. It looked as if they had a fine chance of qualifying for the playoffs. But how far could they go without Le Magnifique? What if Mario was never able to rejoin the team?

As he rested and recovered from his back infection, Lemieux yearned to be out on the ice, but the doctors kept reminding him that he had to take it easy. They didn't even let him resume exercising until almost Christmas. At first he just stretched and tried to build up his strength by riding a stationary bike in the Penguin locker room. He was feeling better and stronger, and the doctors were satisfied with his recovery.

Finally, early in January, they allowed him to begin skating again. Late that month he rejoined the team. In Pittsburgh's last 26 regular season games, he got 19 goals. In

In January 1991, Mario's doctors allowed him to start skating again. Soon he had recovered enough to play in Pittsburgh's last twenty-six regular season games.

the playoffs he scored 16 goals and 28 assists to lead the Penguins to their first Stanley Cup. For that, he was honored with the Conn Smythe Trophy as playoff MVP.

The 1991–92 season held more of the same. Mario took the scoring title back from Wayne Gretzky, with 144 goals, 87 assists, and 131 points. The Penguins had a 39-32-9 season, then beat the Washington Capitals before facing the New York Rangers in the Patrick Division finals.

But early in the second game Mario fell to the ice after being slashed by Adam Graves. A bone in his hand was broken and he had to leave the game. It looked as if he might be out for the season. But with Lemieux watching from the bench, Pittsburgh finished off the Rangers four games to two. The Boston Bruins fell next in four straight games.

That left only two teams—Pittsburgh and the Chicago Blackhawks, who had won eleven straight games. With Mario back in the lineup, Chicago was unable to win a single game in the finals, and the Penguins had their second straight Stanley Cup championship. Lemieux finished the playoffs with 16 goals, 18 assists, and 34 points as he again took honors as the playoff MVP.

The Penguins rewarded him by giving him the richest contract in the history of hockey—$42 million for seven years. If he could stay healthy, they expected him to help them win a few more Stanley Cup titles.

By 1992, there was little disagreement that he was the best hockey player in the world. Lemieux claimed that what he did on the ice wasn't all that hard. "Before I get the puck," he said, "I look where the players are and try to determine where they will be after me. I try to get a crowd to go after me, then pass to who's open. It's easy."

Mario might make it look easy, but that's only because he's so talented. Emile Francis, the former coach of the

The season after their second Stanley Cup victory, the Penguins started off the playoffs by knocking out the Washington Capitals.

Hartford Whalers, said, "He can thread the eye of a needle with the puck. Mario is one of the best passers I have ever seen."

With his long arms and quick moves, he's a tough man to guard. "When he skates with his stick out, there's no way you can reach that far," said Bengt Gustafsson, a Washington Capital center. "And he's so strong you're not going to move him off the puck, either."

Bruin defenseman Ray Bourque said that you have to be very careful guarding him. "If you go at Mario like a madman, he'll make you look like a complete idiot. He just holds the puck out there on his forehand and dares you to commit yourself. If you do, he slips it past you."

But goalies are the ones who have to be especially wary. "You never have any idea what to expect," said Philadelphia goalie Dominic Roussel. "His face is so calm. He shows no sign of stress or anything. . . . It's as if he's saying, 'No problem. Relax. I'm just going to beat you now. It's not going to hurt a bit.'"

Lemieux was beating a lot of goalies during the first three months of the 1992–93 season. After 40 games, he had 104 points. Some Penguin fans predicted that he would break Gretzky's all-time record of 215, set in 1985–86. But then he told team doctors about a lump he had discovered on his neck.

The lump, his doctors decided, was a swollen lymph node. Lymph nodes are found in bunches around the body, especially around the neck, armpit, and groin. Their job is to filter out germs and help the body fight infection. A healthy lymph node is about the size of a bean. Mario's was about the size of a peanut.

After a series of tests, the doctors decided Mario's swollen node was the result of Hodgkin's disease, a type of cancer. Nobody is sure why some people get this disease, but scientists

49

Mario Lemieux's cool expression makes many goalies very nervous. He often surprises them with a quick flick into the net.

are convinced it is not contagious. You can't catch it from somebody else. Hodgkin's disease starts with a swelling in just one node. If it's not treated it spreads to other nodes, then throughout the body. By then, it's a very serious disease. But if the swelling is discovered early, it can usually be stopped.

When he first heard that he had Hodgkin's disease, Mario cried. It was hard to drive all the way home, he said, because of the tears in his eyes. But when the treatments started he was confident. "I've faced a lot of battles since I was really young, and I've always come out on top. I expect that will be the case with this disease."

Throughout his eight years in the NHL, Mario had taken more than his share of bumps, bruises, and injuries. He had broken his hand and smashed a disk in his back. He had also been sidelined by an infection and by bronchitis. But he had always been able to bounce back and rejoin the Penguins.

This time nobody could be sure that he would ever play hockey again. Mario left the team and the swollen node was removed in an operation. Then he began receiving regular radiation treatments to make sure that the disease had not spread. He was placed inside a machine that blasted his upper body with shots of invisible rays. The radiation would temporarily dry out the inside of his mouth, darken his skin, ruin his appetite, and make him feel very tired. But if he was lucky, it would also wipe out all traces of Hodgkin's disease.

Until the treatments were over, he could not play hockey. If the treatments were not successful, he would probably never play hockey again.

51

At only twenty-seven years old, Lemieux was diagnosed as having Hodgkin's disease. Hockey fans feared his promising career might be cut short.

Chapter 7

Mario Lemieux had bigger things to worry about than getting back on the ice with the Penguins: "My health is certainly more important than hockey," he said.

During the next two months he underwent twenty-two separate treatments. He was tired and didn't feel like eating, but after a while he started to feel like playing hockey again. The doctors convinced him to wait until all of the treatments were finished. Finally, on March 2, he had his final treatment. The doctors told him that they couldn't find a trace of the disease in his body. It seemed that he was cured.

Now there was only one thing left to do—play hockey. Even though he felt a little weak and his neck was sore from the treatments, he decided to leave for Philadelphia, where the Penguins would be playing that night. He bought a ticket on a commercial airliner, but bad weather kept the plane from leaving. So Mario chartered a small jet to fly him to Philadelphia. He got there in time for a short nap in his hotel, then left for the Spectrum.

Mario put on a black turtleneck under his jersey so that the collar wouldn't rub against the sore spot on his neck. When he skated out for the opening face-off, the Flyers crowd stood and cheered. Eric Lindros, Philadelphia's rookie star, joined in by tapping his stick on the ice. The words "WELCOME BACK" appeared on the huge screens over the rink. As the cheers grew, Lemieux shyly raised his stick and waved it at the crowd.

By early in the second period, the Flyers had jumped to a 3–1 lead, but then Mario slapped in a goal from the left face-off circle. Fifteen minutes later he slipped the puck to Kevin Stevens, who tied the game 3–3 with a goal of his own.

The Flyers eventually won the game 5–4, but Mario was still glad to be back. "It was a great feeling," he said.

Bill Dineen, Philadelphia's coach, was impressed. "It's amazing. Obviously his heart is in the game of hockey. You've got to give him credit for playing the way he did. You've got to give him credit for showing up."

Lemieux was back and he had played a good game, but would he still be a superstar? Before the cancer scare, his young fans had nicknamed him "Super Mario" after the character in the popular video game. Was Mario still super? It had taken courage to come back so quickly after his treatments, but was his body still up to the challenge? When he had left the team in January, he had been the league's leading scorer. Lemieux had been ahead of Buffalo's Pat LaFontaine by 33 points. When he returned, LaFontaine was 12 points ahead.

As he lay in the hospital for his treatments, Mario had decided that if he could play hockey again he had two goals. He wanted to help the Penguins win their third straight Stanley Cup title, and he wanted to win the scoring championship. He didn't want to come back to the game as

54

just another player. He wanted to come back as *le mieux*, the best.

By April 9, he had erased all doubts. The whole world knew that Mario was still super. Beginning soon after his return, he scored in fifteen straight games. Even though he had missed twenty-three games, he squeaked ahead of LaFontaine in the scoring race. By then the Penguins were the hottest team in the league. They had won all fifteen of the games in Mario's streak. One more win would tie the all-time NHL winning streak.

That night Pittsburgh and the New York Rangers were tied 2–2 after one period. Then Mario went to work. At 4:43 of the second period, he took the puck at the blue line, spun around, and slapped a shot into the net. Less than four minutes later he scored on a long, low wrist shot. Then late in the same period, he took the puck at center ice and headed for goalie Corey

After completing his treatment for Hodgkin's disease Lemieux proved he was still a superstar by scoring goals in fifteen straight games.

55

Lemieux worked hard to overcome his numerous injuries and get back on the ice for the Penguins.

Hirsch. Going at top speed, he faked a shot from the right, then the left. Hirsch hit the ice to block the shot he was sure was coming, but Lemieux still had the puck. Skating past Hirsch, he backhanded it behind the goalie for his third goal. Hirsch couldn't believe the moves he had just seen. "Never in my life seen anything like it. . . . He's an amazing hockey player."

Lemieux had scored a hat trick (three goals) in just one period, but he wasn't finished yet. Hirsch was replaced in the net by Mike Richter, but Mario scored twice in the first eleven minutes of the second period before spending most of the rest of the game resting on the bench.

The Penguins wound up with a 10–4 victory, their sixteenth in a row. Mario, of course, had scored in every one of those games. And after five goals against the Rangers, he now led LaFontaine by 14 points. The Buffalo star had given up hope of winning the scoring title. "Wayne Gretzky was phenomenal," he said. "But Mario is on another level."

The next night the Penguins broke the league record for consecutive wins with their seventeenth, a 4–2 decision over the Rangers. This time Lemieux was held scoreless, but already he and his teammates had their eyes on the Stanley Cup. With the regular season winding down and the scoring title clinched, Mario wanted to make it three championships in a row.

"This is definitely the best team I've played on in my career," he said. And their leader, of course, was number 66. *Sports Illustrated* called Lemieux "the world's dominant pro athlete."

In the 1993 playoffs, Pittsburgh bumped off New Jersey in five games, but was knocked out of the playoffs when David Voiek's overtime goal for the New York Islanders decided the seventh and final game, 4–3.

57

Pittsburgh fans hope Mario Lemieux can continue to bounce back from his health problems. Despite severe back injuries and a life-threatening illness, he remains one of the premier players in the NHL.

After the season, Mario married his longtime girlfriend Nathalie Asselin at the beautiful Basilica of Notre Dame in Montreal. Crowds outside chanted "Mario! Mario!" as the couple left the church.

A month later he had another operation on his back. This one was supposed to repair ripped muscles and remove scar tissue, but Mario's doctors told him that his back was showing signs of degenerative arthritis. Because of repeated injuries, the area around the bones was swollen, and Mario would probably experience constant back pain for the rest of his life.

Despite the pain, Lemieux and the Penguins hoped that his hockey career could continue. He was paid $3 million for the 1993–94 season. If he continued playing, he would get a raise in each of the following three years to $3.5 million, $3.75 million, and $6.5 million. And thirty days after his retirement, the Penguins would give him a $4 million bonus.

But all the money could not make Mario forget the pain. During the 1993–94 season, he was only able to play twenty-two games. In February 1994, he said, "I feel like I'm twenty-eight going on forty-eight. If it doesn't work out this year, I'll think about retiring this summer." Near the end of the season, he told reporters, "My back is more important than hockey right now. My family is more important, my little girl."

Today Mario and Nathalie live with their daughter, Lauren, in a mansion in Sewickley, Pennsylvania, a small town about twenty miles from Pittsburgh. It's a big house with five fireplaces and rooms with thirteen-foot ceilings. Their first home had been in Mount Lebanon, Pennsylvania, but it was quickly discovered by fans. "Everyone knew where he lived," said a reporter. "He'd come out to water the flowers or walk the dog, and he'd have to sign a dozen autographs."

Mario and Nathalie are a quiet couple who aren't usually

seen at parties or in nightclubs. When he's not busy with the Penguins, he's usually playing golf or at home. "I like to relax, watch television, and keep busy around the house," he told a reporter.

Penguin fans, of course, hope Mario will also keep busy on the ice for years to come. And, if he's healthy, that's where he'll surely be.

Career Statistics

Season	Team	League	GP	G	A	PTS	PIM
1981-82	Laval	QMJHL	64	30	66	96	22
1982-83	Laval	QMJHL	66	84	100	184	76
1983-84	Laval	QMJHL	70	133	149	282	92
1984-85	Pittsburgh	NHL	73	43	57	100	54
1985-86	Pittsburgh	NHL	79	48	93	141	43
1986-87	Pittsburgh	NHL	63	54	53	107	57
1987-88	Pittsburgh	NHL	77	70	98	168	92
1988-89	Pittsburgh	NHL	76	85	114	199	100
1989-90	Pittsburgh	NHL	59	45	78	123	78
1990-91	Pittsburgh	NHL	26	19	26	45	30
1991-92	Pittsburgh	NHL	64	44	87	131	94
1992-93	Pittsburgh	NHL	60	69	91	160	38
1993-94	Pittsburgh	NHL	22	17	20	37	32
NHL Totals			599	494	717	1211	618

Where to Write Mario Lemieux

Mr. Mario Lemieux
c/o Pittsburgh Penguins
Civic Arena
Pittsburgh, PA 15219

Index

A
All-Star Game, 31, 37
Art Ross Trophy, 39

B
back injury, 7, 9–11, 41, 43, 45, 51, 59
Badali, Gus, 24
Barrasso, Tom, 39
Basilica of Notre Dame, 59
Boston Bruins, 9, 47
Bourque, Phil, 7–9
Bourque, Ray, 49
bronchitis, 35, 51
Brown, Rob, 39

C
Calder Memorial Trophy, 29
Calgary, Alberta, 31
Canada Cup, 35–37
Casey, Jon, 9
Chambers, Shawn, 9
Chicago Blackhawks, 47
Coffey, Paul, 39
Conn Smythe Trophy, 11, 47
Cullen, John, 9
Cunneyworth, Randy, 40

D
"Dapper Dan Award," 33
Dineen, Bill, 54

E
Edmonton Oilers, 19, 29, 33, 39
Errey, Bob, 7

F
Forum, 14
Francis, Emile, 47–49

G
Gagner, Dave, 11
Graves, Adam, 47
Gretzky, Wayne, 19, 21, 29, 31, 33, 35, 37, 39, 41, 47, 49, 57
Gustafsson, Bengt, 49

H
Hart Memorial Trophy, 31, 35, 39
Hawerchuk, Dale, 29
Hextall, Ron, 40
Hirsch, Corey, 55–57
"Hockey Night in Canada," 16
Hodgkin's disease, 49–51, 53

J
Jagr, Jaromir, 7
Johnston, Eddie, 24, 33

K
Kurri, Jari, 35

L
Lafleur, Guy, 19, 23
LaFontaine, Pat, 22, 54, 55, 57
Laval Voisins, 19–24
Lemieux, Alain, 13, 14, 16, 21
Lemieux, Jean-Guy, 13, 14, 16, 22, 26, 34
Lemieux, Lauren, 59
Lemieux, Nathalie Asselin, 27, 39, 59–60
Lemieux, Pierrette, 13, 14, 16, 22
Lemieux, Richard, 13, 14, 16, 31
Lester B. Pearson Award, 33, 35
Lindros, Eric, 54
Los Angeles Kings, 41

M

Matthews, Nancy, 27
Matthews, Tom, 27
Memorial Cup, 24
Midget Triple A League, 19
Minnesota North Stars, 9, 11
Montreal Canadiens, 14, 33
Montreal, Quebec, 13–14, 18, 24, 59
Moscow, Russia, 22, 23
Mount Lebanon, Pennsylvania, 59

N

New Jersey Devils, 9, 57
New York Islanders, 57
New York Rangers, 47, 55, 57
Notre Dame de Grace Maroons, 16

O

Orr, Bobby, 33

P

Perno, Bob, 24, 34
Philadelphia Flyers, 40–41, 49, 54
Pittsburgh Penguins, 7–11, 24–26, 27–29, 31–34, 35–43, 45–49, 53–60
Prague, Czechoslovakia, 31

Q

Quebec, Battle of, 13
Quebec Major Junior Hockey League, 19–24
Quebec Nordiques, 7

R

Recchi, Mark, 7
Richter, Mike, 57
Roussel, Dominic, 49

S

St. Jean de Matha Church, 14
Sewickley, Pennsylvania, 59
Spectrum, 53–54

The Sporting News, 41
Sports Illustrated, 33, 57
Stanley Cup, 11, 29, 39–40, 41, 47, 54, 57
Stanton, Phil, 9
Stastny, Peter, 29
Stevens, Kevin, 9, 54
Stevenson, Ron, 16–18, 19
Sweden, 23–24

T

Team Canada, 31, 35, 37

U

Union of Soviet Socialist Republics, 31, 35

V

Ville Emard, 14, 17, 26, 39
Ville Emard Hurricanes, 16–18
Voiek, David, 57

W

Washington Capitals, 7, 9, 47
World Junior Champions, 22, 23–24